Original title:
A Necklace of Possibility

Copyright © 2025 Creative Arts Management OÜ
All rights reserved.

Author: Matthew Whitaker
ISBN HARDBACK: 978-1-80586-124-9
ISBN PAPERBACK: 978-1-80586-596-4

The Dance of Future Paths

Frogs in tuxedos jump around,
Twisting paths on squishy ground.
They spin and leap, a merry crew,
Chasing options, shiny and new.

Each step a choice, a tumble, a twist,
In the dance of life, none can resist.
With every chuckle, fortune takes flight,
Turning blunders into pure delight.

Seas of Opportunity

Waves of laughter crash ashore,
Each splash whispers, "There's always more!"
A surfboard made of dreams and hopes,
Riding swells, with fun-filled scopes.

In this ocean, fish wear hats,
Swirling ideas swim with chitchats.
Dolphins dance in endless spree,
Inviting all to surf for free.

Jewel-toned Dreams

In a shop of laughter, colors gleam,
Rings of whimsy, each a dream.
Bracelets of giggles, chains of cheer,
A necklace of fun that's always near.

Every gem tells a silly tale,
Of clowns and cats who dance and wail.
With a wink and a nod, they all unite,
Crafting moments that feel just right.

The Gallery of Dreams

Walls adorned with smiles and schemes,
Portraits glimmer with silly themes.
Each frame a path, painted bright,
And laughter echoes, pure delight.

Art of future, folly on show,
Masterpieces, all a glow.
With every step, a chuckle rings,
In this gallery of wondrous things.

Shimmering Paths

In a world of beads and charms,
Where laughter is the guide,
Each twist adds to the fun,
A wild ride we won't hide.

Juggling dreams like marbles,
With cats always on the run,
We string them up with giggles,
A masterpiece well begun.

They sparkle in the sunshine,
Each choice a quirky dance,
To wear them is to wander,
To dream is to take a chance.

The Tapestry of Choices

In a fabric made of wishes,
With stitches of delight,
Each thread a new adventure,
That laughs into the night.

I once wove a pizza slice,
And a dancing pair of socks,
With a dash of flying fish,
And a hundred joking clocks.

These choices are quite silly,
But they make my heart feel bright,
In this colorful mischief,
Every moment is just right.

Radiance of Aspirations

A star wore my ambitions,
With glitter on its face,
It wished to be a sunflower,
In a never-ending race.

I told it to get ready,
To warp and bend and sway,
Yet all it did was giggle,
And twinkle all the way.

In a garden filled with dreams,
Those aspirations bloom,
With each laugh, the colors shine,
Chasing away the gloom.

Links of Discovery

Adventures await in laughter,
With links of silly glee,
Each funny twist and turn,
A dance for you and me.

We found a hat that squeaked,
And a shoe that liked to moo,
With every step we take,
There's something strange to do.

So let's explore this wacky world,
With each giggle and each shout,
For in the links of fun and joy,
There's never any doubt.

Chasing Illusions

In a world of sparkles and dreams,
I chase the whims and wild schemes.
With a grin, I open the door,
Only to find a rubber duck on the floor.

Thought I'd find fortunes, lush and bright,
But I trip on my shoelace, oh what a sight!
The unicorns giggle, they know my fate,
As I stumble onward, it's never too late.

Adorned with Potential

Wore my best hat to impress the crowd,
But a bee buzzed by, oh so loud!
It landed right on the edge of my nose,
And suddenly I had a fashion pose!

People chuckled at my buzzing plight,
Unaware of the magic in my sight.
With potential wrapped in colors bright,
Who knew fashion could be such a flight?

Lattice of Futures

Picking a path, I twirl and dance,
Each step a chance, oh what a romance!
I conversation with squirrels, they nod with glee,
As they plot their own wild spree.

With each branch crossed, I laugh and sway,
The hilarity grows with each passing day.
In this lattice of life, I trip and twine,
Finding magic in moments, simply divine.

The Elegance of Uncertainty

Dressed in mismatched socks, I step out bold,
With a wink at the world, my story unfolds.
Who knows where this crazy road will lead?
Perhaps to a party with dancing cats indeed!

Each twist and turn, oh what a game,
I'm unsure of the rules, but it's never the same.
In this dance of chaos, I find my way,
With elegance dripping in a comical play.

The Sphere of What Could Be

In a world made of jello, we dance with the flies,
Wearing hats made of fruit, oh what a surprise!
Unicorns in pajamas, they flutter and fling,
While we juggle our hopes like a clown with a swing.

From bubbles of laughter, dreams start to rise,
With rubber duck friends, in a splashy disguise.
We leap over rainbows, and slide down the sun,
In a land where the silly is all about fun.

Radiant Possibilities

A fish wearing glasses recites Shakespeare's lore,
While llamas in tuxedos tap dance on the floor.
We ride on wild turtles, with socks on their shells,
Exploring the humor in whimsical spells.

With candy cane trees and ice cream for skies,
There's giggles and snorts and some very odd cries.
An orchestra of frogs serenades from the bog,
Life's best opportunities are found in a fog.

Kaleidoscope of Dreams

A chicken on roller skates zips by with a grin,
While otters are hosting a wild tofu kin.
With pixie dust sprinkles, we scatter our fears,
And drink fizzy laughter like fine nectar beers.

Unruly balloons float and start to debate,
About the best way to navigate fate.
As cats wear capes and fly high like kites,
The mischief of dreams rules our giggly delights.

Echoes of Uncharted Routes

An octopus barber is styling my hair,
While rainbow-eyed fish play truth or dare.
In the land of confusion, we laugh with pure glee,
Jumping puddles of jelly on our tiptoes with glee.

With cakes that sing songs and clocks that rewind,
We venture through lands that are one of a kind.
Each corner unveils a peculiar sight,
As we frolic and skip into the whimsical night.

Artifacts of Desire

In a dusty drawer, treasures lay,
Each one a dream, in disarray.
A rubber band, a spoon, a shoe,
All hold stories, if only they knew.

Trinkets and tokens, a jumbled mess,
They whisper wishes, with no need to stress.
A paperclip bends to hold it all tight,
Oh, the nonsense can sparkle so bright!

Twists of Fate

A shoelace crossed, oh what a sight,
Tripping my friend, with joyful delight.
We laugh as we stumble, no fears on display,
For fate's little gags make life more of a play.

A cat on a roof, oh what a pose,
While he dreams of fish, we give him a nose.
Twists of calamity, we dance with our quirks,
In each silly moment, the universe smirks!

The Weave of Hopes

Threads of confusion, all intertwined,
Hopes like spaghetti, so twisted, aligned.
In the kitchen of wishes, we boil and we bake,
Creating a masterpiece—oh, what a mistake!

We dabble in jumbles, a knitting delight,
With yarns that collide, it's quite a sight.
All tangled together, yet perfectly fine,
A jumble of dreams, all dressed up in twine!

Lanterns of Opportunity

We carry our lanterns, all lit with flair,
Glowsticks and giggles, in the night air.
We dance through the shadows, in the bright light we trust,
Finding paths in the dark, it's a whimsical must!

A glow-in-the-dark necklace, a beacon of cheer,
With laughter and mischief, we draw near.
Each flicker a chance, to stumble and sway,
Lanterns of laughter, guiding our way!

Shards of What's Possible

In a world of plastic dreams,
My hope is made of cheese.
Wobbling like a jellybean,
It bounces on the breeze.

I found a fortune cookie,
But it only gave me gum.
With a splash of whipped cream,
Life's a silly drum.

A cat in a top hat,
Dances through my thoughts.
He twirls and sings a ditty,
While I give him some quarts.

Laughing at my blunders,
Like juggling marbles loose.
Each slip a little treasure,
With luck, I make a moose!

Threads of Serendipity

In a closet full of socks,
I found a sparkly shoe.
I wore it on my head,
And danced a jig or two.

A pancake on my forehead,
Promised syrup from the sky.
With a grin and a wink,
I gave it all a try.

Rainbows in my cereal,
Flavored like surprise.
Each spoonful tells a story,
Of secrets in disguise.

With every silly whimsy,
Let curiosity thrive.
Embrace the joyous puzzling,
And really feel alive!

Potential in Every Glimmer

In a garden of lost keys,
I found a golden ball.
It whispered funny secrets,
And didn't bounce at all.

A spoon with dreams of travel,
Claimed it ranked a prize.
Each sip of silly nectar,
Sweeter than the lies.

A feather turned magician,
Conjured up some stew.
With laughter like confetti,
It cooked up something new.

So gather all the giggles,
And sprinkle them with cheer.
In every tiny moment,
Potential's always here!

Serenity of Choices

In the garden of delights, I choose my fruit,
A pineapple hat and a clown shoe boot.
Every peck and poke raises a joyous cheer,
Options abundant, like socks with no peer.

Sipping lemonade from a fancy glass,
Tripping over daffodils, oh what sass!
Each path I stride down could lead to a pie,
Or a dance with a llama, oh me, oh my!

Veins of Promise

In a creek of chances, I plunge my feet,
Wading through puddles, oh, life's quite a treat!
A jester on stilts serves me cotton candy,
While singing about dreams that are always handy.

With glittery fish swimming past my face,
Every splash a giggle, every wave a race.
A world so bright, painted with sheer delight,
Making tomfoolery an everyday rite.

The Symphony of Aspirations

Bubbles of laughter rise on the breeze,
As toads in tuxedos croak with such ease.
Harmonious hopes on a merry-go-round,
Conducting a giggle, a simple sound.

Each note in this place dances like a cat,
And the butterflies hum while twirling with that.
Life's a mad concert, each aria fun,
Where even the shadows are never outdone!

Glints of the Unforeseen

Twinkling surprises light up the street,
A unicycle dog with a heartwarming greet.
Each detour I take brings a quirky unfold,
A treasure map left by a pirate, so bold.

With marshmallow clouds drifting past overhead,
I bounce on the grass, springing dreams into thread.
Each glimmer a chuckle, each shimmer a wink,
I dance with the sparkles and tiptoe on ink.

Circles of Dreamweavers

In a land where socks dance free,
The dreamers weave with glee.
They string the stars on pie,
While frogs sing lullabies.

With a wink and a swirl,
They spin dreams in a whirl.
Wishes bounce like rubber bands,
As giggles fill the lands.

Mice wear hats and twirl around,
Each step a joyful sound.
A cat serves tea to a mouse,
In this whimsical house.

In circles, they laugh and play,
Crafting dreams day by day.
With sparkles, laughter, and cheer,
They turn the world, oh dear!

Beads of Ambition

Beads of jelly on a string,
Dreams are sweet, let's take a swing!
A pickle joins the parade,
In this quirky escapade.

With vibrant colors, they shine bright,
Each bead a wish takes flight.
A banana's doing the cha-cha,
While unicorns sip on soda.

Ambition dressed in polka dots,
Hoping talent's what it's got.
Guitars made of macaroni,
Play tunes that are rather phony.

Let the magic bring a smile,
As we strut our funky style.
With laughter sparkling like dew,
In this world, dreams come true!

Cascades of Wonders

In a forest where dreams cascade,
Wonders leap in a parade.
A squirrel wears a tiny crown,
As fairies twirl round and down.

Chocolate rivers sway and flow,
With candy trees all in a row.
A bridge made of bubblegum,
Makes us dance, oh so dumb!

Dancing in the moonlight's glare,
With marshmallow puffs in the air.
Each step a springy delight,
We giggle into the night.

Cascades form with each surprise,
As magic twinkles in our eyes.
The wonders of this joyous spree,
Celebrate our wild jubilee!

Whispered Horizons

On whispered winds, ideas flit,
Like cheeky birds that never sit.
Horizons stretch with silly cheers,
And we conjure up our fears.

Marshmallows riding on a breeze,
Tickle our toes, oh yes please!
The sun wears shades, what a sight,
As we dance with sheer delight.

A jellybean's salute to yonder,
While pumpkins sing with eyes of wonder.
Whispers of joy through the night,
With dreams that twinkle so bright.

At horizons where laughter flows,
Adventure blooms, and friendship grows.
With giggles far and near,
Life's a song we hold dear.

Whispers of the Untold

In a drawer where dreams collide,
Lies a treasure where laughter hides,
Sparkling gems of unlikely tales,
That twinkle bright like happy snails.

Each shine a story, quirky and bold,
Of dancing socks and birds in gold,
Little whispers, secrets unfold,
In every laugh, a mystery told.

Bumblebees in tuxedos prance,
While turtles in shades invite you to dance,
Join in the fun, don't miss your chance,
In this world of whimsy, take a stance.

Life's oddities across the miles,
Wrap you up in vibrant smiles,
Discover the joy in every miss,
And treasure what the world might kiss.

Silk Ribbons of Chance

A ribbon tied to a swinging door,
Leads to a place where silliness soars,
Cats in top hats, dogs on stilts,
Giggles unravel, spun from silk quilts.

With every turn, surprises await,
Like spaghetti boats on a chocolate lake,
Join the circus of stardust and glee,
A parade of joy, just you and me.

Jump in a pool of rainbow sprinkles,
Dance with the stars, hear the twinkle,
A world where socks always have mates,
And laughter is served on banquet plates.

So grab a ribbon, take a wild leap,
In a carousel of hopes, no need to keep,
For in this adventure, we all enhance,
With threads of humor, let's take a chance.

The Essence of Dreamscapes

In realms where squirrels wear capes of red,
And jellybeans dance in your head,
Giggles are currency, smiles the gold,
In dreamscapes where antics unfold.

Unicorns trumpeting the silliest tunes,
Bounced along by bright, silly moons,
Where cupcakes bloom on candy canes,
And fog whispers love through cottony lanes.

Tik-tok clocks tick with ludicrous glee,
While pixies help paint the sky by decree,
Each brushstroke giggles with colorful flare,
As dreams become moments, wild and rare.

So leap into visions with open delight,
In a land where the absurd feels so right,
Embrace the funny in all that we chase,
And dance through the essence of whimsical grace.

A Tapestry of Wishes

Weaved with threads of bright yesterdays,
A tapestry sways in quirky ways,
It tells of wishes that giggle and wiggle,
In colors that jump, twist, and jiggle.

Whimsical frogs in oversized shoes,
Play hopscotch with whispers and silly clues,
Each patch a tale of laughter and cheer,
With winks and grins that pull you near.

A blanket of dreams patterned with glee,
Where wishes float like ships on a sea,
They sail with laughter, wild and free,
At the whim of the wind, just let it be.

So stitch your hopes with a giggle or two,
Immerse in the fun, let your spirit renew,
For in this tapestry, love strings along,
A symphony of joy, silly but strong.

Gems Beneath the Surface

In my backyard, I found a gem,
A shiny rock, not worth a dime.
I wear it proudly, my hidden stem,
Creating stories with every rhyme.

Neighbors tease, they call me daft,
My treasures made from bits of clay.
But in my heart, I know the craft,
Turns simple stones to grand ballet.

I polish these with laughter bright,
Pretend to own a world so rare.
They sparkle soft in morning's light,
My jewels play without a care.

Each chip's a laugh, each crack a joke,
Who needs the fancy shine of gold?
With every step, a wild stroke,
My silly gems, forever bold.

Mirror of Infinite Paths

In a funhouse, mirrors twist and shout,
Each curve a dream, a silly fate.
I see a traveler—what's that about?
Flipping shadows at a rapid rate!

Reflections dance, they trick my mind,
One's a hero and another, a cat.
Each glimpse, a giggle I can find,
In this maze where logic falls flat.

I wave to friends, but they just laugh,
As they trip on paths that bend with glee.
We're lost in curves, a merry staff,
Mapping laughter, wild and free.

Each turn we take, our dreams collide,
With silly faces, fun's not far!
In this fun mirror, joy's our guide,
Creating paths where we all spar.

Glimmers of Tomorrow

I sprinkled dreams like fairy dust,
Hoping for glimmers just around,
But found a shoe, a sock, and rust,
Tomorrow's glimmers rarely found.

With every step, my fate's a game,
Today's odd finds, tomorrow's glee.
Each mishap brings a well-earned fame,
Turning socks into a tapestry!

Glimmers shine where laughter lies,
A hope that's more than just a prank.
In chaos, truth brightly flies,
A treasure chest in every bank.

So here's to dreams that go awry,
The best surprises are wrapped in cheer.
With every trip, I dare to fly,
Yesterday's trouble, today's frontier.

Basket of Possibilities

I found a basket, frayed and torn,
It holds my dreams, each silly thought.
With crushed-up hopes, like breadcrumbs worn,
I wonder what wild schemes I've sought.

I tossed in wishes, silly whims,
And plucked out giggles, packed them tight.
With every poke, the basket grins,
Each laugh a star that twinkled bright.

When clouds roll in, I sift through dreams,
Each possibility, a feathered jest.
Sometimes it's dog hair, or moonbeams,
Yet in this chaos, I find my rest.

So here's my basket, full of cheer,
Each whimsy woven, laughter's tune.
In every twist, the path is clear,
To find the joy beneath the moon!

The Glow of What Could Be

In a room of mismatched socks,
I ponder 'What next can I rock?'
The fridge hums a curious tune,
As I dream of dancing on the moon.

Worms with glitter, frogs in capes,
Inventing new forms, wiggles, and shapes.
A hat made of cheese, how fun, it seems,
Is this the world or just my dreams?

The clock strikes twelve, time's a fun prank,
Dancing on beams, what's next in the tank?
With friends made of giggles and ice cream cones,
We're crafting adventure, just follow those tones.

Laughter is currency, don't be shy now,
Let's trade silly tales, I'll show you how.
With a bounce in our steps, we float like a kite,
In the glow of endless, wondrous delight.

Harmonics of Uncharted Dreams

Whispers of jokes float on the breeze,
As I juggle my thoughts with virtual cheese.
My cat sings the blues, in a karaoke bar,
While wishes ride unicorns, oh, isn't life bizarre?

We dance on the edge of a pineapple slice,
With clowns in top hats rolling dice.
Creating symphonies from spaghetti strings,
Each moment a melody, see what it brings.

A world where ducks wear sparkly ties,
Where bubbles are dreams, floating high in the skies.
On legs made of noodles, we tiptoe on air,
Concocting new wonders, a whimsical affair.

The snort of a giggle, the howl of a cheer,
Paints all our moments, brightening the sphere.
Together we're wild, with hearts open wide,
In this concert of laughter, we joyously ride.

Chains of Serendipity

Tangled in laughter, the days become threads,
Linking small mischiefs, like pearls in my head.
A teacup full of giggles, just spilled on my shoe,
And who knew that sneakers could be worn with a tutu?

Cupcakes like clouds float up toward the sun,
While squirrels wear bling, thinking they're fun.
In a world made of jelly, we bounce and we sway,
As the oddest of creatures come out to play.

Stuck in a loop of loop-de-loops,
We tumble through life with jumping poodles and scoops.
With a splash of confetti, we make every day,
An adventure in silliness, hip-hip-hooray!

Our chains made of dreams, no room for despair,
With buddies who chuckle, they brighten the air.
Life's a crazy puzzle, just join in the spree,
With laughter as glue, we're forever carefree.

An Ember's Journey

A spark in my pocket, oh what a tease,
Flames made of giggles dance with the breeze.
Set off on a quest for the silliest rhyme,
As I hop through the forest of sweet, sticky slime.

With marshmallow trees that sway to the beat,
I frolic with critters in shoes made of meat.
The sun wears a smile, the moon is a wink,
And the stars tell us secrets we silly folks think.

A rolling cupcake causes a stir with a cheer,
As the world spins around, we've no room for fear.
On cushions of laughter, we float through the night,
Chasing our dreams until morning's first light.

So pack up your giggles, this journey's a blast,
With playful reminders, let's make the fun last.
With flickers of joy lighting up the whole way,
An ember's adventure is here to stay!

A Cascade of Potential

In a world where dreams can sway,
I found a hat that danced away.
It wiggled left, then to the right,
A feathered friend, what a sight!

I wore it high; my head was spun,
Rabbits joined, oh what fun!
They laughed and raced, a joyful chase,
In this hat-world, I found my place.

With shoes that squeaked and socks that glowed,
Every step was a laughter code.
Jumped over puddles, splashed the ground,
In this zany spree, joy was found.

So here's to dreams that woosh and whirl,
Where laughter sparkles like a pearl.
Embrace the silly, dive right in,
For in this world, we all can win!

Reflections in a Shimmering Sea

On a beach where shadows dance,
I found my luck in a jiggly prance.
A crab in shades chased a seagull,
They bumped and tangled; oh what a hull!

With sandcastles built in crazy forms,
We made a fort to weather storms.
But waves laughed loud and tumbled through,
Our palace bright became a stew!

Seashells whispered secrets so unclear,
"Wear us as hats, make the world cheer!"
I twirled around, a beachy mime,
With sunscreen smears, we danced in time.

So here among the waves and glee,
Life's a dance on this lively spree.
With each reflection, laughter leaps,
In this shimmering sea, joy keeps!

Threads of Infinite Journeys

With threads that sparkled in the sun,
I stitched a path, oh what fun!
Each loop a giggle, each knot a cheer,
I wove a tale that drew us near.

My sewing skills, a bit askew,
A button popped; it flew and flew!
Chasing after it, I lost my shoe,
But oh, my friends, there were quite a few!

In this fabric world of colors bright,
Tangled up, we danced in delight.
Safety pins became our crowns,
Wearing giggles stuck in frowns.

So let's embrace this fabric spree,
With stitches that sing of joy, feel free!
In threads of laughter, we will play,
Unraveling fun, day after day!

Pendants of Luminous Fate

In a market bright, where wonders gleam,
I found a charm that made me beam.
A pendant shaped like a giant pie,
Said, "Wear me, kiddo, reach for the sky!"

But as I twirled it, it danced away,
Bouncing on clouds, oh what a display!
A cat in boots joined the chase,
"Let's catch that pie, it's our saving grace!"

Through whirlwinds of laughter, we flew high,
With a spaghetti lasso, we aimed for the sky.
But this pie laughed, too cunning to catch,
Leaving us giggling, a glorious batch.

So here's to charms that giggle and sway,
In life's great circus, come what may.
With pendants bright and fate's embrace,
Find joy in every playful trace!

Lumens of the Future

In a world where dreams run wild,
The future's bright, like a playful child.
With sparkly lights that wiggle and twist,
We chase our hopes, we can't resist.

Fates are like socks that rarely pair,
A clown's pink nose, a wobbly chair.
Balloons that float on a sunny breeze,
Tickling our minds, oh, such a tease!

Time's a jester, with tricks up his sleeve,
He makes us chuckle, oh let's believe!
Each twist and turn, a silly surprise,
In a quest for the stars, we aim for the skies.

Fragments of Bright Paths

Shiny pebbles on a winding road,
We stumble and giggle, oh what a load!
Each tiny fragment, a piece of cheer,
Twinkling bright, drawing us near.

Socks on our hands, we dance like a fool,
In puddles of laughter, we splash like a pool.
A maze of nonsense, the map's upside down,
With every wrong turn, we wear a big frown.

Through tickles and jigs, we leap and we bound,
In our whimsical quest, happiness found.
Each step an adventure, with stories to share,
In this fragment of life, we're free as the air.

Echoes of Hope

There's a bounce in the air, a skip in our shoes,
With echoes of laughter, we sing out our blues.
A wild serenade of hope that we crave,
Like jellybeans jumping, so bold and so brave.

A wiggly worm on a sparkling day,
Calls out to the sun, come out and play!
Dancing with shadows, we twirl like the leaves,
Laughter is magic, the heart that believes.

In the echoes of joy, we find a bright tune,
While riding the laughter, we soar like a balloon.
With whispers of dreams, our hearts start to glow,
In the echoes of hope, together we flow.

Mysteries Woven in Light

In a tapestry stitched from giggles and glee,
Mysteries dance, oh come here and see!
With threads made of sunshine, we weave our delight,
Chasing the shadows, from morning till night.

A cat wearing boots, strutting down the lane,
Makes us all chuckle, oh what a gain!
With colors exploding like fireworks in bloom,
Our lives are a circus, with joy as the room.

The riddles of life, like balloons that we chase,
Each twist and each turn, we find our own space.
In mysteries woven, our happiness glows,
With laughter as fuel, our adventure just grows.

The Radiant Scroll of Potential

With every twist, the scroll does spin,
A tale of laughter, let the fun begin!
Each loop a giggle, each fold a cheer,
Unraveling mysteries, joy draws near.

What if my cat wore this funky flair?
With jewels of jellybeans, oh, what a scare!
Dancing through dreams, they prance and play,
With a wink of whimsy, they lead the way.

A rubber chicken hangs from bright gold thread,
A shining beacon, all worries shed.
With playful gems, the world's a stage,
In this scroll of potential, we laugh and engage.

So let's hang dreams, from ear to ear,
With sparkles of laughter, spread holiday cheer!
For each glimmer tells tales we can weave,
In this radiant scroll, watch us believe.

String of Dreams

On a string of laughter, dreams are strung,
Like bouncing bunnies, forever young.
Hopping through hopes, we giggle and sway,
As wishes glide by in a silly ballet.

Imagine a llama with a sparkly tail,
Jogging in socks, setting off on a trail.
Each step a giggle, each bounce a shout,
In this string of dreams, we dance about.

A quirk of fortune tied in a bow,
A unicorn sneezes, and oh, what a show!
With laughter as colors, and silliness bright,
We weave through our dreams, pure delight.

So grab hold your yarn, let's twirl and spin,
With joy as our guide, let the fun begin!
For on this string, our hopes do gleam,
In this tapestry bright, we laugh and dream.

Threads of Tomorrow

In threads of tomorrow, we stitch our fate,
With laughter and puns, we create our state.
Each fiber a joke, a tickle, a tease,
Sewn moments of joy are designed to please.

What if the sun wore a polka-dot hat?
And danced with the moon while chitchatting with that?
The stars chuckle softly, 'It's quite the display!'
In these threads of tomorrow, we're free to play.

A patchwork of giggles, stitched with a rhyme,
We craft our adventure, one day at a time.
So let's spin our yarn with a giggly twirl,
Embracing the fun as our dreams unfurl.

In these threads, we find a whimsical space,
Where laughter and joy leave a sparkling trace.
So come take a ride on this laughter ship,
And sail into tomorrows where we'll never slip.

Gemstones of Hope

In pockets of giggles, the gemstones lie,
With each silly sparkle, they lift us high.
Colors of laughter, in joy they gleam,
Shining bright promises, like a happy dream.

A ruby red clown nose, jiggly and round,
Whispers of joy sing a silly sound.
With emerald wishes and sapphire grins,
In this gemmed comedy, the fun begins.

If hope wore a tutu and danced on the moon,
Would it giggle and chortle, singing a tune?
With lighthearted banter, we stand, we cheer,
In this world of gemstones, let's spread the cheer.

So let's treasure each moment, each giggle, each hope,
With these precious charms, we can soar and cope.
For laughter's the magic, the spark in our eyes,
In these gemstones we see, our joy never dies.

Fragments of the Ideal

In a world of cotton candy dreams,
Where unicorns balance on vibrant beams,
I tripped over thoughts dressed in sprinkles,
Caught in a laugh, where reality crinkles.

A penguin in a tux, what a sight!
Dancing the tango in the pale moonlight,
Wobbling here, flapping there with glee,
Who knew absurdity would set us free?

A sandwich of wishes on a plate so grand,
Served with a side of laughter's band,
Each bite a giggle, each crunch a cheer,
Dining on dreams as we hold them dear.

So gather the wild, the odd, and the rare,
Collect moments that dance in the air,
For life is a jest, a playful ballet,
In the fragments of dreams, we twirl and sway.

The Fabric of What-Ifs

Stitched with a thread of quirky delight,
The fabric of thoughts keeps me up at night,
What if cats could really pilot planes?
Or if jellybeans washed away all pains?

A tapestry woven with colors so bright,
Trips to strange lands where odd doesn't bite,
A quilt of conjectures, soft on my bed,
Sometimes I nap in the dreams in my head.

Say, what if trees wore shoes and a hat?
Would squirrels throw parties where all would chat?
Would raindrops dance to old jazz tunes?
Or sing with the stars, under moonlit dunes?

So let's gather the silly, the giggles, the fun,
And weave through the day under a whimsical sun,
For life is a play, full of whimsy and laughs,
In a fabric of what-ifs, we craft our own paths.

Crystals of Tomorrow

In a shop of wonders with shelves piled high,
I found glimmering dreams, catching my eye,
They whispered of futures where all things gleam,
And I laughed at the silliness of every dream.

Would toast toast to a slice of pie?
Or would chickens up and start to fly?
Imagine the skies filled with froggy balloons,
Bouncing around while humming sweet tunes.

With crystals of laughter and sparkle of cheers,
We'll chase down our hopes, dispelling all fears,
Each shimmer a chance to dance and to play,
In the playground of life, let's frolic away.

So gather your giggles, your sparkles, your fun,
For tomorrow's bright glow has only begun,
With every wild dream that we dare to embrace,
We'll wrap up our worlds in a glittery case.

The Art of Being

In the gallery of giggles, where laughter resides,
The art of being spins in jubilant rides,
Where paint splashes joy on the canvas of time,
And silly tickles make the heart feel sublime.

What if clouds dressed as fluffy white sheep?
Or turtles played cards for a chance at a leap?
Each stroke on the canvas, a burst of delight,
As we weave our own tales, day into night.

So paint me a picture of whimsical dreams,
With colors that twinkle and sunlight that beams,
For in the gallery of life, let's wear our bright hues,
Create our own fun in the most splendid of views.

In the art of being, let's frolic and dance,
Chasing the wonders with each happy glance,
For joy is a masterpiece, waiting to see,
What magic unfolds in the art of just being.

Thread of Dreams

In the attic, I found a thread,
Stitched with giggles, bright and red.
I thought of clouds and cupcakes too,
As it wove a path, oh what to do!

I pulled it tight, it snapped just right,
A jumpy tune flew out of sight.
It danced around like a bumblebee,
And laughed aloud just to tease me!

With every tug, a joke appeared,
The kind that leaves one's thoughts quite smeared.
Like socks that hide and play a game,
This thread of dreams has no real shame!

So let's weave tales that make us roar,
With every stitch, we demand more!
In a world where laughter sets us free,
Oh, what a thread, it's so carefree!

The Adorned Horizon

The horizon wore a silly hat,
With feathers bright and a dancing cat.
A sprinkle of stars, oh what a sight,
It hummed a tune that felt just right!

Each sunrise laughed, a bright parade,
While coffee beans joined the charade.
They skipped and frolicked with glee,
As the horizon sang, 'Come dance with me!'

With grapes on vines, that danced and twirled,
They created joy and laughter swirled.
A world adorned with silliness,
That promised to leave us in pure bliss!

So grab your hat and join the fun,
Let's whisper secrets to the sun!
On this horizon, bold and bright,
We'll spin and twirl with sheer delight!

Glistening Paths of Tomorrow

I walked a path with shoes of light,
That glimmered bright with pure delight.
The ground below chuckled in glee,
Said, 'Who knew you could dance like me?'

With giggles and sparks lighting the way,
The future whispered, 'Let's play today!'
A bubblegum tree grew lifted high,
As birds wore hats and began to fly!

Each turn I took, a surprise would spring,
A rubber duck that began to sing.
It quacked a tune that made me laugh,
As I strolled down this quirky path!

Tomorrow's roads are paved in cheer,
With jellybeans lining the way, my dear.
So let us giggle, let us sway,
On glistening paths, come what may!

Charms of the Unseen

A box of charms sat 'neath my bed,
Filled with giggles and dreams unsaid.
I opened it wide, not knowing what,
To find a cat in a polka-dot!

Invisible friends began to play,
Juggling rainbows, so bright and gay.
They tossed their giggles to the sky,
As flocks of squirrels began to fly!

With every charm came a funny tune,
That made a cake dance with a spoon.
Balloons floated, each with a grin,
As we celebrated, let the fun begin!

So if you hear of unseen charms,
Just know they're stirring up some alarms.
Delivering laughter directly to you,
In every glance, the charm shines through!

Labyrinth of Alternatives

In a maze of choices, I roam about,
Each turn I take, there's laughter, no doubt.
Pick a snack, or wear a hat?
Life's odd twists, like a dancing cat.

Shall I dance with a broom or ride a cow?
What a wild life, I get to enjoy now!
Flip a coin for breakfast, eggs or toast?
A breakfast feast that's worth a boast!

Every option twinkles with glee,
Like a puppy chasing its tail, can't you see?
Should I sing or become a tree?
The possibilities are endless, whee!

In this labyrinth, where shall I go?
Monkey bars or a limbo show?
Choices galore make me grin so wide,
In this playful maze, I'll slip and slide.

Chimes of the Unexplored

What's behind the door? A dancing ghost?
Or perhaps a feast of buttered toast?
With every chime, the laughter grows,
Unexplored wonders in whims and throes.

Shall I wear socks that clash with my shoes?
Or juggle pies—oh, which one to choose?
Knocking on doors, no telling what's found,
Prancing like a penguin, joyfully unbound!

Every new sound is a curious bell,
Telling tales of a life lived so well.
Should I skip or slide down a hill?
In this circus of life, I fit the bill!

Whirling around like a spinning top,
With each twist and turn, I can't stop!
The chimes ring out with untold delight,
In the dusk of my dreams, I take flight.

Trellis of Wishes

On a trellis where dreams intertwine,
I wish for pickles and some vintage wine.
Will I leap or simply trip?
A journey begins with a silly flip!

What if a giraffe decides to dance?
Or I wear pajamas to a fine romance?
Every vine with laughter, oh what a scene,
With wishes blooming, like bright jellybean.

Should I paint my house in polka dot hues?
Or wear a cape while I knit my shoes?
Swinging on a wish, with a laugh on my face,
In this world of whimsy, I find my place.

Each wish is tangled, like a knotted string,
But the joy they bring makes my heart sing.
On this trellis, I'll plan a parade,
With giggles and fancies, nothing will fade.

Bright Horizons Ahead

As I wake to the shimmer of dawn's bright light,
I ponder the choices that spark delight.
Should I wear stripes or polka dots today?
Each horizon beckons, come out and play!

The sun can't help but giggle and grin,
Telling me tales from the world within.
Maybe I'll ride on the back of a whale,
Or sail through the sky, on a colorful sail!

Every new day is an open door,
Filled with adventures and giggles galore.
Should I climb a tree or catch a breeze?
Life's little moments just aim to please.

With bright horizons calling my name,
I'll step outside and join the game.
Counting clouds, trading wishes up high,
In this fun-filled dance, I'll learn how to fly!

Embers of the Unknown

In a pocket I found a key,
It opened a door, but what's the fee?
A cat in a hat with a cup of tea,
Said, "Join me for fun, or just flee!"

With a wink and a grin, she danced around,
Spinning tales where lost socks abound.
Who knew in the dark, such treasure is found,
With giggles and secrets, our laughter unbound!

I stumbled upon a box of old shoes,
Each one a story, each pair some muse.
Should I wear the red ones, or stick with blues?
In this thrift store of life, there's always a fuse!

So here's to the paths that lead us astray,
Chasing down rainbows that lead us to play.
In the ashes of doubt, let's bright spirits sway,
With a spark of the unknown, we'll dance all day!

Echoes of Promises

I promised to bake some cookies today,
But only the flour flew wild in dismay.
Eggs took a flight, what a messy display,
Now I've got cake, or so I will say!

The oven's a monster, it roars and it shouts,
While mixing the batter, I spin and I pout.
But out pops a treat I can't live without,
A gooey surprise that my dog's found out!

With sprinkles and smiles that glitter and shine,
We share bites of laughter, a drink of good wine.
Promises made are just silly designs,
In the kitchen of life, let's savor the lines!

So gather around while the chaos is ripe,
In echoes of joy, let flavors entice.
Cook up some fun, add a dollop of hype,
In the mess of our making, we find our own spice!

Chain of Endeavors

Linked arms and wild dreams, we take to the street,
Spinning adventures like candy to eat.
In each jazzy step, there's a funky beat,
The chain of our laughter is quite the treat!

On this journey we wear mismatched shoes,
Exploring the paths where curiosity brews.
With glances exchanged and creative views,
Our hustle becomes an amusing ruse!

We chase after rainstorms and dance in the mud,
Loyal companions, we're bound by the thud.
With each little bump, we dive in the flood,
Creating our destiny, wild and unstud!

So let's toast to the moments that bind us in glee,
In the chain of endeavors, there's boundless esprit.
With joy and mischief, we'll each be the key,
Unlocking our futures, forever carefree!

Charms of Change

In a town where the clocks often jump and jive,
I found a strange potion that made me alive.
Every sip brought a giggle, a wiggle, a vibe,
With charms of change, oh, how we'd thrive!

A hairdresser's cap with a magical comb,
Transformed all my locks, said, "Make this your home!"
Now I strut like a peacock, no need for a dome,
With colors and sparkles, I'm free to roam!

Magic escalators that lead me astray,
Each twist in the tale feels like child's play.
With wind in our hair, let's dance in the fray,
In the laughter of change, we joyfully sway!

So here's to the whims that tickle our sides,
To the charms of the world where our spirit resides.
In the landscape of fun, let's embrace all our rides,
For the change that we cherish is where joy abides!

Refractions of Light

In the prism of laughter, colors collide,
Bouncing off walls with nowhere to hide.
Every giggle a facet, perfectly bright,
Reflecting our quirks with delight in the night.

From the silly to crazy, a spectrum so wide,
Shining through moments, our joy we can't hide.
Twinkling like stars, or maybe a bug,
We cherish these rays, wrapped up in a hug.

Glowing in chaos, we dance through the day,
Chasing reflections that lead us astray.
Who knew there was humor in light's little bends?
Laughing together, where the fun never ends.

So catch all the colors that scatter around,
Embrace all the weirdness, let laughter abound.
In a world like a rainbow, we playfully sway,
Making memories bright in a colorful way.

Mosaic of Life's Wonders

Each piece tells a story, so quirky, so grand,
A tile made of chaos, a splash of demand.
In a kitchen of dreams, mix laughter and spice,
Crafting our tales, every slice is precise.

Building a puzzle of giggles and cheer,
Some fragments are gold, while others, oh dear!
With glue made of charm, we stick it all fast,
Creating a canvas that's fun to the last.

From socks that don't match to the dance of a bird,
Collecting odd moments, the loud and the absurd.
A patchwork so vivid, it's hard to ignore,
Life's wonders are wacky, but who could want more?

So gather your bits, your snickers, your sighs,
Every jumbled-up piece makes the brightest of ties.
In the mosaic we share, together we thrive,
A colorful journey, that's how we survive.

Loom of Possibility

On the loom of our dreams, we weave with a grin,
Threads of the bizarre, where nonsense begins.
Each twist and each turn, brings a chuckle or two,
Creating the fabric of 'what if' with you.

With fibers of whimsy and patterns of cheer,
We stitch up the moments that bring us near.
A tapestry tangled, yet charmingly bright,
Crafting the wild tales that dance in our sight.

So grab a few strands, let's tangle and play,
In this fabric of fun, we'll find our own way.
Creating connection through giggles and knots,
Laughter's our loom, tying up all the thoughts.

Let's wrap up our wishes in silks of delight,
Each stitch is a memory, a flicker of light.
In this whimsical project, dear friends, take a chance,
Together we'll weave our own silly dance.

Golden Threads of Thought

With thoughts spun like gold, all shiny and bright,
We wander through dreams, on paths full of light.
Each idea a giggle, a twist of the mind,
In the treasure of nonsense, true golds we will find.

A quicksilver whim, a sparkle or two,
The laughter we share becomes art to renew.
Knots tied with humor, as bright as a flare,
We decorate thinking, with joy in the air.

So take all your ponderings, tangle them well,
In the fabric of friendship, let's weave a great spell.
The threads of our thoughts, both light and bizarre,
Create a nice tapestry, shining like stars.

In this quest for the silly, with joy as our guide,
We're stitching together, with laughter applied.
So here's to the threads, shining bright in our minds,
In the loom of our dreaming, pure fun we will find.

Radiance of Neverland

In a land where dreams run free,
Pirates dance with glee, you see.
Crocodiles wear fancy hats,
And fairies chat with sassy cats.

Balloons float up to the moon,
Twirling clowns sing silly tunes.
Flying fish in rainbow shoes,
Swim through skies, oh what a muse!

Wishes wrapped in candy bright,
Found at dawn, then lost by night.
Juggling stars upon a beam,
Living life within a dream.

So grab your hat and join the fun,
A wild ride has just begun.
In Neverland, we laugh and play,
Chasing giggles every day.

Embrace of Limitless Skies

Kites that giggle in the breeze,
Whispers shared between the trees.
Clouds in pajamas float on by,
While owls laugh and wink an eye.

Sunshine sprinks joy like confetti,
While silly squirrels dance all petty.
They throw a party on the hill,
With acorn cups and laughter's thrill.

Rainbows juggle with no regrets,
As unicorns play poker bets.
With pencils twirling, dreams take flight,
Creating chaos, pure delight.

So let's pretend, just for today,
That skies are filled with frolics, hey!
In every giggle, joy complies,
With magic floating in the skies.

Fragile Links to Infinity

Tiny baubles, sparkly and bright,
Dance in shadows, a playful sight.
With every twist, a giggle sings,
As jellybeans sprout tiny wings.

Butterflies gossip, sharing the tale,
Of chocolate rivers that never pale.
Marshmallow clouds roll through the sun,
As donuts glide, oh what a fun!

Silly thoughts spin in circles fast,
Catching laughter, what a blast!
Wishing wells toss sparkles high,
While hiccuping frogs leap and fly.

So come along, let's weave and bend,
With fragile links that never end.
In every chuckle, life is free,
Building dreams like a silly spree.

Ornaments of Soon

In a world where time stands still,
Jesters bounce and whirl at will.
Eggplants wear the finest clothes,
And broccoli, well, who really knows?

Tomorrow's treasures wait with cheer,
Wrapped in giggles, fringed with fear.
Gummy bears plot to take their stand,
While lollipops form a marching band.

Silly hats piled high and wide,
Decorate the fun we bide.
Penguins tap dance on the sand,
As tickled turtles lend a hand.

So here we stand, in a funny tune,
Crafting smiles with the gift of 'soon.'
In every shimmer, joy is found,
Let's make the world a laughter ground.

Jewels Beneath the Stars

Under the night so bright,
I found a gem of delight.
A sparkly rock caught my eye,
It winked at me, oh me, oh my!

I thought I'd wear it, just for fun,
A diamond doorknob, oh what a run!
It rolled away, like it was on track,
Who knew jewels had such a knack?

I searched the grass, I trod so slow,
Chasing brilliance, what a show!
I tripped on laughter, fell with glee,
And giggled at my clumsy spree!

In the end, with dirt on my face,
Who needs jewels when you've got grace?
The stars all twinkled, they surely saw,
My treasure was joy, without a flaw.

The Locket of Intentions

I found a locket in a lost and found,
It whispered secrets, oh what a sound!
Inside, I saw my wildest dreams,
A chocolate fountain, or so it seems!

I wore it to prove I'm profound,
But tripped on shoelaces, fell on the ground!
The locket laughed, it did a jig,
I wondered if it knew my gig!

I took it off, it giggled loud,
Now I'm the fool, not so proud.
Intentions mixed with whimsy's dance,
My locket loves a playful glance!

Tracking wonders, oh what a quest,
It's all so silly, but I love it best!
The locket stays, my friend in woe,
Together, we'll put on a show!

Beads of Hope and Wonder

In a jar of beads, I reached so deep,
Each one a wish I tried to keep.
A blue for laughter, red for cheer,
Oh, I should wear them? Sounds like a idea!

But as I strung them on one sparkly day,
I knocked the jar; what a display!
They rolled like marbles, wild and free,
Crafts gone wrong are just meant to be!

A cat dashed by, a colorful race,
Chasing beads all over the place!
I laughed so hard, I lost my breath,
These beads brought life, more than death!

In the end, I made a crown,
Mixed-up colors, a silly gown.
Donning chaos, oh what a sight,
I'm queen of fun, all day and night!

Ties That Bind the Unknown

A rope of dreams, all twisted and tied,
Whisk me away on a wild, swift ride!
My shoes were tied with a ribbon of fate,
Let's see if it leads to a magical date!

I wandered around, with no sense of time,
Tangled in laughter, it was sublime.
But alas, my shoe came undone,
I stumbled and fell, oh what fun!

Spinning like tops, we laughed until dawn,
With ties so quirky, we were never withdrawn.
Banana peels, oh what a sight!
I slipped and slid, but felt so light!

So take a chance, let threads interlace,
Life's a giggle, enjoy the race!
With every trip, I sing my tune,
In the ties that bind, we'll find the moon!

The Compass of Ambitions

In the land of dreams, I twirl and spin,
With a map all drawn, I just can't win.
The arrows point straight, but I veer away,
Chasing after squirrels, oh what a day!

I plotted a course, it seemed so clear,
But a pizza truck came, and now I'm here.
Navigating toppings, with anchovies rare,
A navigator's nightmare, but I don't care!

Each time I ponder, my plans go a'fling,
Like that kite in the wind, oh what a fling!
Dreams take a turn, and yet I just grin,
For in every detour, a new laugh begins!

So here's to the chaos, the laughs we create,
With every misstep, I celebrate fate.
My compass just spins, oh what's the right way?
Oh look, there's a donut! I think I'll stay.

Silk Threads of Imagination

With scissors in hand, I snip and I clip,
Creating a world with a colorful zip.
Spinning such patterns, in my mind they dance,
Twisting and turning, oh what a chance!

A quilt made of giggles, with starlight seams,
I patch up my hopes, with threads of big dreams.
But every time I try to make sense,
My cat takes a leap, it's all so intense!

I woven a tale with bubblegum glue,
Flashing a smile like the sun shines anew.
But wait, here comes trouble, like socks without mates,
My imagination bursts, it just can't wait!

Tangled in laughter, I trip and I fall,
On feathers and sparkles, oh look, what a ball!
My fabric of thoughts, it might seem unkempt,
But in silly delights, my heart is exempt.

Ornaments of the Future

With glittery dreams, I bang pots and pans,
Creating my fortune with funky old cans.
Shiny and bright, they dazzle my eyes,
A piñata of wishes, oh what a surprise!

I've built a tall tower of wishes and hopes,
Out of marshmallow fluff and coat hangar ropes.
Each ornament shines, but some wobble and sway,
Oh no! Down it goes, like a cat in a fray!

With laughter as glue, I attach a big grin,
These knick-knacks of wisdom, where do I begin?
A hat made of dreams and a tie made of fun,
Decorated in puns, oh look, the day's won!

So let's hang our quirks on the tree of today,
With ornaments dancing in the silliest way.
I'll hoot like an owl, and the stars will both sing,
For life's all a circus when you're wearing a ring!

Veils of Potential

Behind every curtain, there's something to find,
A jester that juggles, with laughter entwined.
Balloons float above, with wishes like clouds,
While puns and giggles escape from the crowds.

Each veil a riddle, each twist a delight,
With silly surprises that tickle the night.
I peek through the layers, and what do I see?
A disco-ball dragon, oh, let's set it free!

Wearing a crown made of cupcakes and cheer,
The future shines bright like a chandelier.
With every layer peeled back in glee,
I discover my spirit dancing with glee!

So let's lift the veil, and let's spin and sway,
With laughter and joy, it's a bright, silly day.
For potential's not pressure, oh no, it's a game,
Where fun leads the way, and the laughs are the same!

Array of Dreams

In the land of socks and shoes,
I found a fish that loved to snooze.
It dreamed of dancing, bold and free,
With jellybeans as company.

A hat that says 'I'm quite absurd',
With every twirl, it spins a word.
A world of waffles, pies that sing,
Oh, what adventures dreams can bring!

Balloons that float on silly strings,
Whisper tales of kings and things.
A cat who juggles all day long,
Pondering where the cupcakes belong.

With every wish upon a star,
Hoping for adventures near and far.
A treasure map marked 'Take a chance,'
Inviting all to join the dance!

Twinkling Moments

Once I stole a moonbeam bright,
Wore it like a hat of light.
It danced atop my head with glee,
As I pulled pranks on the nearest tree.

A squirrel wore shoes two sizes big,
And ran a race with a stubborn pig.
They laughed so hard, they both turned pink,
Who knew a farm could smell like ink?

Cupcakes rapped to the beat of time,
With sprinkles that would often rhyme.
My toaster started up a band,
Toasting tunes that were truly grand.

So gather 'round, let's share a cheer,
For wacky moments stay right here.
With laughter woven through our days,
We'll make each moment sing and play!

Bracelets of Mindfulness

I wore a bracelet made of dreams,
Each bead was stitched with silly schemes.
It whispered secrets, quite absurd,
To ponder life, when pranks occurred.

A rubber chicken joined my wrist,
It quacked out wisdom I can't resist.
Stretching time with every giggle,
Turning stress into a wiggly wiggle.

Jellybeans slip through fingers light,
Offering smiles both day and night.
Each charm a memory, wild and bold,
Like treasure maps we love to hold.

With mindful laughs, and sunny plays,
We'll bridge our thoughts in funny ways.
In every bracelet, joy abounds,
Collecting laughter from our grounds!

The Paradox of Aspirations

I aimed to fly like a dancing leaf,
But stumbled over my own belief.
Turns out dreams have their own ploys,
Sending me tumbling, oh what joys!

A toaster wished to be a queen,
Serving waffles, crisp and keen.
Yet every time it tried to reign,
It burned the toast and caused some pain.

A treadmill aims to take a break,
And stretch its legs—what a mistake!
It dreams of running in the park,
But gets stuck playing hide and spark.

So here we are, with plans in mind,
Where laughter and chaos intertwine.
Embrace the odd, let freedom sing,
In whims and dreams, we find our wings!

www.ingramcontent.com/pod-product-compliance
Lightning Source LLC
Chambersburg PA
CBHW070311120526
44590CB00017B/2627